August Codde

The Existence of God attested through the Marvels of Nature

August Codde

The Existence of God attested through the Marvels of Nature

ISBN/EAN: 9783337210571

Printed in Europe, USA, Canada, Australia, Japan

Cover: Foto ©Lupo / pixelio.de

More available books at **www.hansebooks.com**

THE
EXISTENCE OF GOD

ATTESTED

THROUGH THE

MARVELS OF NATURE.

(FIRST EDITION.)

By AUGUST CODDE.

DETROIT, MICH:
M'CORMACK PRINTING COMPANY, JEFFERSON AVENUE.
1883.

[Entered according to Act of Congress, in the year 1883, by AUGUST CODDE, in the Office of the Librarian of Congress at Washington, D. C.]

Sold by W. F. HELLWIG, 115 Rivard Street, DETROIT, MICH.
CODDE BROTHERS, 87 Randolph Street, DETROIT, MICH.

NOTE.

These poems, before they were printed, were read by several men of education and good Christians, who urged me to have them published. They considered the work to be very interesting to all persons, and tending to edification, and hoped for it a wide circulation. That these objects may be attained—for they depend on each other—is the wish of

THE AUTHOR.

PREFACE.

The object of this little work is to show the Existence of God attested through the Marvels of Nature, the first work brought to light by the author, and, being written in clear language, it may all be well understood. It is not composed for contradiction, for this would be unwise; in other words, the Gospel should not be reversed or denied. Our holy fathers, through the holy Apostolic Church, have shown in an admirable way, to infidels, that there is a God without beginning and everlasting, having an almighty power and wisdom. Yea: a Creator who made Heaven, firmament and world in perfect order by pronouncing the word. A Lord who made the body of man from dust, animated it with an invisible and immortal spirit, as it were a spark of His divinity, one day to return to Him; that He instituted laws, through words and acts, to warn and strengthen him against sin. Those laws, well known, are convincing to man if he is good and willing, and trusts in his Divine Master.

The sun, moon and stars show brilliantly His glory, even the earth and sea proclaim God's existence, and cause His beauty to bloom. Can we, then, deny this, or should we doubt that the angels in Heaven sing constantly with the greatest pomp and devotion, *Gloria in Excelsis Deo!*

The Lord, sitting upon His throne, throws an eye of mercy, to share with man, according to His promise, an everlasting and magnificent happiness; but, alas, if we refuse His grace and offerings we will suffer the consequences, although the powers of Heaven will not cease.

Moreover, to begin since the new era—the birth of our Lord Jesus—joy and glory came from Heaven and shone on earth through the air upon men of good will. The redemption of man was at hand. He was that holy seed promised by God to Adam since his fall, to crush the serpent's head. It was through the same God of Abraham, Isaac and Jacob, the God of angels and prophets, the Father of all men, that our blessed Redeemer was sent to lead all the souls of the just to eternal happiness, and to teach and save sinners by marvelous acts, instruction and suffering. It was He who brought light into the world and opened Heaven. His holy life personally on earth, although now nearly past nineteen centuries, to-day is fresh and brilliant, and devotion to His Holy Name and Sacred Heart is still increasing. And the very same precepts and words He spoke are taught through the world by the ministers of His Church. We know the Son of the Almighty God required nothing of this world, not even the dust which covered his garments after His daily labors. He was inflamed solely by divine love for the salvation of man. His wisdom and mercy were boundless. The poor He fed, the sick He cured, the dead He revived. Yet His people denied Him. He was flagellated, crucified and died a most cruel death.

The Lamb of God embraced every humiliation, to fufill His mission, and to obey His Father's will, although He was all powerful. His divinity shone through His many mighty miracles, but He never put His hand to those who bound Him, nor even spoke a harsh word to those who scourged and spat at Him, but prayed for them. He said: "Father, forgive them: they know not what they do." Although we know, the whole world with its contents is at the mercy of His hand or word, the sun, moon, stars, tempest, earth and sea obey His voice, and Heaven shows His Godly majesty, and that naught is impossible for Jesus.

O man, can we forsake Him, or shall we deny His instructions, His prophecies and miracles, which were partly to be seen in Jerusalem, and which are every day of such great interest for mankind? His words and acts are remembered, recorded, conserved and printed in all languages, translated with the greatest care and bound into the most lustrous books. Yes, to-day, His glory, His majesty, His Divinity reign, and are among rational beings of great consolation through Godly grace. Which must teach us all, that a father of a family who neglects to keep the Life of Christ under his roof to lead or to improve his own career, or to teach his children the path of virtue, is considered unworthy of the name of Christian.

Now, dear brethren, if we cannot deny Jesus Christ, we dare not deny His Father in Heaven. Man, being the work of the Almighty God, must embrace humiliation;

he must consider himself in comparison with the majesty of his Maker, as a drop of water against the sea, a spark of fire against the sun, a little grain against the whole world. When infidels once come to this conclusion, they will know the value of a man made of dust, and cease to criticise God's works or to deny His existence. They will feel happy, and humble themselves, and say they were ungrateful to protest against the wisdom and goodness of their Creator; they will proclaim that conversation which tends to degrade the name of God is blasphemous and merits punishment even here on this earth. Yes, they will feel it their duty to confess that he who denies the existence of God, or declares that all that exists is derived from itself, must be a fool.

The author hopes, that if now and then he has used any harsh expressions, it will be forgiven him; for, when speaking or writing on subjects of such importance as religion, charity commands men to utter the truth frankly and fairly in the plainest language. He believes that no man on earth will feel annoyed or chagrined at him for expressing, in a public manner, the fact of the Existence of God attested through the Marvels of Nature, for he does so only in a charitable spirit, to prevent errors, desiring to benefit and to exalt his brother men to the dignity for which we were created.

THE AUTHOR.

THE EXISTENCE OF GOD

ATTESTED

THROUGH THE MARVELS OF NATURE.

PART I.

O man, although we are deprived to see the Lord,
We must observe His laws, His name should be adored!
Since Heaven and world were made by superhuman hand,
A master must control the sky, the sea and land.

The firmament, no human sense can comprehend,
From time 't was truly made is firm, obedient,
It teaches upright men to honor here, their God,
As their Creator dear, who made them from a clod.

The sun, a bright, celestial fire, shines night and day;
Supplies mankind with gifts and comforts on their way;
All nature through his sparkling rays spreads out in bloom,
And cherishes all creatures, freeing them from gloom.

The moon, refulgent mirror sweet, reflects at night,
The navigator's friend, from ocean tells the tide;
Her wondrous course, so changeable. is fairly led;
To prophecy the times, her golden rings are spread.

Unnumbered stars, embellishing the heavens, so clear
All show a mighty hand to souls upon this sphere,
Appearing every day, and always full of glory;
To tell their substance here below, is but vain story.

The earth, though seeming dead, for man is kind and good,
She lets him toil the ground, produce abundant food.
Each race receives its share, to dwell exempt from cost:
The harvest stands secured 'gainst storm, severest frost.

Oh, powerful the seas, which spread from pole to pole!
Show waves to swallow up the whole earth, roll by roll!
But when to force their prisons, efforts are in vain,
Well knowing from the Lord permit they must obtain.

Their waters moisten earth, the fish are kept and fed,
And many precious things are found, and widely spread;
All through the earth to man they lend a friendly hand;
To help him in distress, the sea vies with the land.

The brutes all dwell upon the earth to favor man;
To him their labor free present as much they can.
Convincing fact, as mule and horse will prove indeed,
Their mouths on purpose made to bridle them in need.

God made man last, with soul to His own taste and will,
The world intrusted him, besides His treasures still;
Surpassing nature's laws, all through sweet intellect,
A spirit purely cast, God's kingdom to protect.

The soul, an ornament to God's Divinity,
Far, far above the firmament in dignity;
Has to return to God, to join the saints and blest,
And, serving Him, it cannot fail with Him to rest.

Without the soul of man, world never would exist.
Man should know this, and not the Lord's commands resist;
And thus he lose his soul, so everything be lost—
No treasures found to pay for what his spirit cost.

Behold, since sun, moon, stars, brutes, plants the earth and sea,
To benefit all men are made and to agree,
Obedient then should we be unto God our Lord,
Nor violate his rules, nor ill-use Heaven's support.

Man is endowed with precious gifts as nature's king;
Not to destroy his Maker's work, sweet offering.
Nor infidel should be, denying truths and facts,
But should defend his dignity by Godly acts.

If we revolt 'gainst God, who for us spared no cost,
Our hearts then sure through vicious trespasses are lost,
And acts and deeds profane as raging fire would spread,
More innocents from their good principles be led.

A man denying God ne'er was a Christian's friend,
His object to degrade God's name, His laws to rend,
And bribe an honest man; but 'twill not be allowed,
For reason will announce that God he disavowed.

His teachings may appear mankind to patronize,
But overthrow God's Church, and His name scandalize.
He would try to assure that world shall never end,
Sun, stars above, men, brutes below, in chance all blend.

But what would atheists say in teaching such a tale,
If Christians of a simple matter gave detail,
That Peter's picture all was finished in one night,
Without a brush and paint, no painter's hand to guide?

They surely would declare such man to be insane,
Yet more—great foolishness such questions to explain.
For paint and brush can make no picture, show man's face,
Without the painter's hand—ne'er was there such a case.

Still atheists will utter words, yes, foolish talk,
Comparing man to ape, the first on earth to walk,
His shape in time improved, effect of sun and air—
Shall Christians suffer such canards and call them fair?

The ape improved him (sophists say) like man does now;
But if he did, he always would be monster low,
And barren as the seeds of grafted plant or tree,
To disappear as snow-flakes, never more to be.

Some say the insects have begotten Father Ape,
Uniting sense and frames, they thus have wrought his shape;
When he was changed to man he lost his hide and tail,
Became full intellect—was it by storm or gale?

While other sects say, they believe but what they see;
But what they see is hard for them on to agree.
Though they ne'er saw man ape, can it be understood
That they believe such trash, diverting men from good?

It seems to be ridiculous on apes to speak,
Our brethren to defend now being lost and weak;
Although Americans, a civilized, wise nation,
Yet find men to devise such hateful degradation.

How pitiful for man on reaching olden year,
Remaining in that class who God's wise works impair!
A sacrilege it is, comparing human soul
To apes or brutes; oh, can such men their hearts console?

All that existed once, are yet and will remain;
No changes to man known forbids him to explain.
The truths of God by Noe were spoken pure and clear,
We should not doubt—he is of Christ third figure dear.

The infidels must fail with reason to explain,
And Christian men will not their schemes corrupt sustain;
For parents giving ear drive children to despair,
In Satan's sphere to suffer everlasting there.

Those schemes foretold are cruel, destructive to mankind;
Alas, poor child, if being taught such faith to mind!
No Godly peace exists to man who God denies;
He loses Heaven, the Lord's sweet mercy to despise.

Man through such acts his soul debases 'neath the brute,
For brutes fulfill God's will without one to dispute;
The pagans, too, are better—they adore the sun,
Or something God has made, or through His word is done.

For eye has witnessed not that apes engendered men,
Nor horse became a cow, nor even frog a hen,
Unaltered apple trees produce a plum nowhere;
Alone is this enough to call such talk unfair.

All race and fruits us show t' exist from world's begin,
Our forefathers have seen like we see now therein.
Invention will not hurt God's works, which show so bright.
Experience teaches us from Heaven comes all the light.

The forest men uncivilized we must deplore,
But even they by smoke of pipes their God adore,
And, having kings, obey, keep up a rule and fame,
Surpassing apes and brutes, although they might be tame.

Now, friends, we being brothers dear in Jesus made,
And well instructed, should despise not God our Head.
The angel guardians then would leave us unprotected.
God's wrath so near, He might destroy us unexpected.

PART II.

The man who teaches that no Heaven and Hell exist
Will foster criminals, his passions not resist;
Then Satan's slave, is apt to curse his father, mother.
Can he be justly called a loving son, a brother?

He wants to overthrow the laws of God and state,
Although we need God's law world's laws to operate.
'Tis often shown, when man the fear of God has lost,
To rob or kill his master little pains it cost.

Consider man's career, who leaves his wife and child,
He causes grief, distress, his heart with passion wild;
The name of God he will despise, and mock His Heaven,
Ungrateful for all blessings daily to him given.

Examine man's belief who burns his neighbor's home,
Or kills his landlord through the night in his own room.
A man we often find who loud denies creation,
And, being God's great foe, has bloody inclination.

Ask you the lad his faith, committing parricide,
He will reply, no faith—but God he will deride;
Because his schooling was, When thou diest all is death,
The body being flesh, the soul is but a breath.

When highest court is to decide upon divorce,
A father, mother comes without the least remorse,
Protesting 'gainst true faith, Christ's Church they scandalize,
Deprived of charity, they scorn to compromise.

'Tis true, bad men exist, once raised in holy creed,
But, through gross sinful acts, they lost their faith indeed.
See: faithful Christians will observe God's rule and law!
When Satan finds no room he must his snares withdraw.

Behold, the judge in court calls God to hear the truth,
He knows without God's fear no evidence, in sooth;
In order well to show that lies do injury,
Imposes sentence most severe for perjury.

Can infidels, then, keep a place of trust or fame,
Before God testify, if they deny His name?
It would destroy all right, produce a mocking act,
And through injustice lose the clearest case in fact.

This brings in mind and view God's law was first to lead,
For Heaven's happiness man followed it—we read.
This shows God's laws and man must work in harmony,
Which clearly is expressed in sacred history.

Absurd to call the spirit of departed wife,
To drive one's business on, to know what will arrive,
And yet deny the Maker, Heaven, Eternity,
Ignore the sou.'s abode, its rights and dignity!

Is't not absurd to trust horse-shoe above the door,
To keep the Devil out, or have good luck the more;
And openly deny Almighty God our Lord,
Who made all that exist complete for man's support?

Is man not cursing God to say He never was,
And call God's children fools and of the lowest class?
Again—if God exists, to be a cruel ghost,
Creating fire intending men for sins to roast?

Such men would not object if Heaven was—not Hell;
They would then live at ease, rule wickedly full well.
But all must know, our Lord wants both, his right to show,
To give the just His Heaven and bad men Hell below.

The scale for justice's sake we might here well compare,
If sins exceed good works, must sacrifice repair.
An homicide is hanged or prisoned is for life:
Those pains are justly dealt, for Judge no blame or strife.

How many times we hear a criminal offender
Is forced from hands of law (refusing to surrender)
And hanged? This bloody act is not allowed—should fail;
Though justified his doom, for sins press down the scale.

Our Lord is far more kind to all, it seems not strange;
For men deserving death, He waits, asks them to change;
But, when abusing, sends His messenger to say,
So many days are left you to repent and pray.

Oft lives of atheists are cut off by God above,
For He has touched their hearts and shown them mercy, love;
They promised to repent, but, habits being strong,
Die sudden in despair, before restoring wrong.

The state of man in life when conscience has been lost,
Is like a ship disabled, finds no more the coast;
Then, dragged by heavy waves, its thorough wreck is sure;
Experience teaches clear, hard fate it will endure.

The infidels call man's race most intelligent,
Coax him to mock his God, to grow wise, opulent;
The Church and priest, they say, keep man a slave—and more.
How can they know? they never tried the truth before.

No profit 't is for egotists to sing such song,
But Christians pity them; they must to Christ belong;
By loving, serving God, may enter Heaven's gate.
They cannot choose the world for their celestial state.

All know that man on earth is not full satisfied,
For he is made for Heaven, and God's laws must abide.
Christ says, "Good servants will enjoy most happiness,
Receive reward eternal in the land of bliss."

'Tis wrong to say that plows surpass most humble prayer,
That in great famine 'twould show man took better care.
The plows were used where most destructive famine struck,
How was the harvest lost, how came then such bad luck?

Perhaps the reason was they gave ear with delight,
To heretics, or men defending Satan's "right,"
Where poisoned seed was spread among some Christian youth,
And thus destroyed God's fear and love, and, and lost the truth.

The infidels all would believe if our good Lord,
Would send more miracles—His acts would be adored.
But they profess to be so wise and sound of mind,
Their Maker yet deny—it shows how they are blind.

They would abuse the Lord more than Arabians,
Whom atheists call dunce below the Indians;
For trusting Christ, who cured the lame, revived the dead;
Yet those men saw them walk, and one took up his bed.

Can infidels hate men who follow Christ's advice,
Who sweet instruction brought from Heaven, to world's surprise?
He clothes the naked, cures the sick, and feeds the poor.
Shall we refuse poor old men bread or shut the door?

They will hate Christian souls as they hate God above,
Though Christians teach us all as brothers each to love,
And watch the children to preserve their innocence,
T' obtain God's grace, beg Jesus' Mother's influence.

They ask new miracles, for those of Christ are old,
And there are some each day; but 't is as Jesus told.
He said: "They all have eyes to see, but acting blind,
And ears to hear, pretending deaf, they will not mind."

Although to God the cause that some are deaf is known,
Why they reject their Saviour's gospel to them shown,
Which would instruct so wisely through pure holy creed,
No more to insult their God by any word or deed.

The Christian mothers are opposed to infidels,
They know their word against God's wondrous works rebels,
And call them dressed-up wolves in sheep or young lambs' hide,
Their children to devour or drive to Satan's side.

The Christian daughters will refute the bad device
Of that lost man, and cannot follow his advice,
Because deceitful 't is and ruins men below,
And serves eternal happiness to overthrow.

What would the doctors say in practice for years past,
If tailors, blacksmiths, all would claim it fair at last,
They should instruct the doctors medicines to use?
Would they not call them fools such project to induce?

We might the more term fools, who try to change God's word.
From early times some made sham creeds, without accord;
But they are all condemned—their act now clearly tells,
"Reforming" drove them all to join the infidels.

THROUGH THE MARVELS OF NATURE.

Though men deny their God, the Heaven's power sublime,
Still, not content, they seek a higher, nobler clime.
Behold, to find a God they search all through the skies,
With their balloons they soar thro' many glorious dyes.

But how can God be found amid the star and cloud,
By wandering souls, denying Him, rebellious, proud?
The nearer they approach the canopy of Heaven,
The more their strength abates, the less God's view is given.

Their ships are sent to poles to see the world suspended.
In vain all efforts are, there's nothing apprehended.
From year to year the lives of thousands are destroyed;
Because they disbelieve in God all acts are void.

They know before they start no man can find that way,
And yet, though well convinced, they try without delay;
But, since opposed to find their Maker's light sublime,
The search can do no good, 'tis all but losing time.

If true Divinity should not exist in fact,
Then man must understand the skies, and how they act,
And guide the seasons all to his own taste and will,
Control the cyclones, all that is unpleasant still.

He should command the sun, the moon, the stars new courses,
Repulse the water from the mounts, the hills and sources,
Cut off the fury wind its strength all through the air,
Destruction to prevent which whole world has to bear.

But no: when earthquakes throw the world in fearful state,
He feels 'tis not men's power such cause to operate,
But work of our Almighty God, whom some deny,
Who has in hand all lives, at will can make them die.

The very times the mounts and plains are trembling fast,
Then great fear fills their hearts, they cry and pray at last.
Oft water, fire, are thrown from out the depths of earth,
To swallow up estrayed men, who but Hell are worth.

Since world's beginning wonders have awaked man's race—
Destruction may occur if we misuse God's grace;
But, while surrounding facts surpass our intellect,
We should a Master trust, His plans the best respect.

PART III.

A man denying Heaven or God's omnipotence,
Must show some documents to argue in defense;
But previous to Noe no writing's found on earth—
Can infidel explain what there before took birth?

Then naught but foolish pride must govern that man's mind,
To teach erronèous creeds, for which no base we find.
What benefit to him the Christians to mislead?
The snares he lays for them, will catch himself indeed.

Those wandering men have judgments different in kind:
Some disbelieve in God, have nothing on their mind,
While others blame men loving Jesus crucified,
Although the Son of God for our salvation died.

Some say, "If God exists we could not praise His laws,
Because for Adam's sin our children not the cause;"
And yet an unjust man is punished often here,
Which causes pain to his own child, though young and dear.

Experience all we meet, surrounds us everywhere!
Regard a father having children in his care:
If he his earnings waste, by conduct lose his fame,
His children sure will suffer—but, were they to blame?

Suppose a father by misconduct lose respect,
His child will lose esteem, and deep on it reflect;
It may be virtuous, but stains will dwell within,
Preventing it the place its father lost by sin.

A child who through his father loses fear of God,
Dwells in a dangerous state, for vice obstructs its road;
'T will serve as tool and nail to build its father's bier,
And hasten his last days, wish him to disappear.

What Adam lost, man too, hath lost, beneath the skies,
Though noble happiness was given in Paradise;
But justice all divine was through man's sins provoked,
He punished him, those graces previous given revoked.

Th' idea that man should deny the Infinite,
Because he does not see Him, sense will not permit.
If he believes but what his weak eyes witness here,
Defense he has not, cannot claim to be sincere.

Since truths and facts with brilliancy show clear and sweet,
Man's sense should mind, apply God's grace his case to meet.
To this undoubtedly good virtues are required,
And to be Christian, from all unbelief retired.

By walking into groves and fields in early spring,
He sees the plants are small, the ground but covering;
When summer's noon approaches all is spread in bloom,
Thus promising man's food for winter soon to come.

No doubt, these plants and trees have called his mind in spring,
Now bearing, but no eyes saw grow or move a thing.
While generating acts of nature blind man's eye,
We must submit to God, his loving child to die.

A pure, refreshing dew is there in early morn,
Its substance hard to tell or see how it is born.
It is not water, neither rain, and yet its taste
Is wanted for all kinds of fruits—none can be waste.

The gales and stormy winds, so powerful but light,
Unseen, all dominate the air—can crush in might!
They do not hurt the plants, to leave man good supply,
Oh, what nice mysteries—his soul to edify!

Since saints and martyrs all God's gospel full sustain,
Whose lives through wisdom, charity in bloom remain;
We should not trust these quarrelsome, deceitful men,
Who God's sweet words deny or holy works disdain.

To rule Almighty God, or not his works sustain,
Is mockery—opponents cannot right obtain;
A child insulting God, the best of fathers dear,
Must be insane or lost to wholesome love and fear.

What! great inventors' works are all to be denied,
Because the maker was not known and since has died,
And when his titles like his works show true and clear!
'T is wrong to say, they came alone upon this sphere.

Man, if thine eyes are wickedly to govern thee,
Then never shalt thou change a soul of God to be;
If grateful were thy heart thou wouldst not strive in vain,
For witness through created things thou canst obtain.

O man, incredulous, denying God and faith,
What will awarded be to thee at hour of death,
If thou forsak'st the truth? thy eyes and sense deceive,—
When all corrupt is, can the soul its loss retrieve?

He who sustains corrupt news publicly exposed,
Will teach it to his friend, who, too, will be imposed.
Fly him, for truly he is but a foe to men:
He cares not if you enter Heaven or Satan's pen.

A man protesting God cares not man's laws to mind,
And gospel truths inside his heart no room can find;
Though clearly do they show God's power, clemency,
And give man happiness, destroy insurgency.

Some say: "If God reigns, ministers should perfect live,
Instead of breaking rules; yet oft they scandals give."
But, friend, take their advice, when they God's word explain,
And notice not their acts if they not good remain.

Hark! If thy brother sin, let not thy heart be torn;
The sole reward would be for evermore to mourn.
Is man not wrong to take his life and jump in Hell,
Because his friend did so, with whom he used to dwell?

We should all watch, well knowing man subject to fail.
If trusting, loving God, we never would assail;
Let's toil our vineyards, for good fruits we must obtain!
E'en good land when neglected will produce no grain.

We see good things on earth, the heavens in harmony,
They all instruct God's children, feed their memory.
And open roads of grace, e'en leading to the sky.
They say: "Call on your God, there's plentiful supply."

Do not ignore, Christ mourns if men by sin offend,
Though always ready when the souls are sick to mend;
At once we should repent, if on the wicked way,—
Good Heaven us will support to see a brighter day.

To this we must give God our hearts and fruits we gather,
In pure and lowly way, like children to their father;
Then sure our race will follow, form a Paradise
On earth, and happiness will reign, to world's surprise.

When we are but awaked by thunderclaps or wind,
Our soul not pure enough, 't is doubtful God to find.
Hence love is more desired, esteemed above world's fear,
Then God will bless those men—pure souls to Him are dear.

Alas, when nature quakes, all hearts will faint away!
Then, sinners, to call God is but a poor essay;
Man's pains will interrupt his prayers when death is near:
We should good Christians be before great risks appear.

When during life entire, man was against his Master,
Will he then call for help to free him from disaster?
Suppose he, through excitement, supplicate God's grace,
Shall His sweet clemency descend his dreary place?

Our Lord might hear man call in thunderstorm or flood,
But knows when call's sincere (this must be understood).
Perhaps God made him many urgent calls before;
His thanks were sins on sins against Him more and more.

Let's give our souls to God ere on death-bed we lay,
For now our minds are strong to drive the fiend away,
And, cleansing souls so late, it may not be sincere —
Nay, strength too weak with serious works to interfere.

Let us consider well, in God we all must trust,
A Father, Maker dear, created us of dust;
That His beloved Son, Jesus Christ, has left His throne,
Through whom salvation to good-willing men is done.

PART IV.

A true wise man will not debase the works of God,
But, praising them, will send great thanks to Heaven's abode;
He knows that sinful acts destroy reward and trust,
Denying Jesus and the price His blood has cost.

Without this faith man's sense grows dim, admits temptation,
He will neglect good works and lose his destination;
And evil hearts will watch, in darkest spot remain,
To steal their neighbor's purse or goods, if chance obtain.

When man denies his God he is deprived of fear,
And when no sins exist, may kill his brother dear;
Where God dwells not we find no love, no charity,
And men to Satan sold hate Christian unity.

When man believes and says the world itself conducts,
Frail nature contradicts his words, them Heaven obstructs.
If world shows each society requires a head,
Then God must govern Heaven, world, living men and dead.

O foolish man, to alter what surpasses sense,
Or to explain by tricks those mysteries immense!
God's works are strange, 't is true, but 't is His holy will;
Although not satisfied, we must endure them still.

But atheists, wonder 't is, want to attack a God,
Destroy His works, seduce man from salvation's road;
And yet God patiently keeps up their lives so sweet.
They should their own works test if anxious faults to meet.

A child shall never run until it moves to walk,
And neither shall it speak before it tries to talk;
Men, therefore, should not read, but first learn A B C,
Else tunes would discord prove and be no harmony.

That works above exist beyond man's sense to reach,
Shows us a head supreme is there man well to teach;
As here, if man's unable to discern a plan,
He asks an explanation of a wiser man.

Let us not criticise sweet Heaven, but view the ground;
See from one kind of sap how many fruits are found!
We profit all of these; in strength are kept alive,—
Can we explain, how from these flesh and blood derive?

And seeds so simple, but how wonderful the mold,
When planted in good ground produce an hundred fold;
The tender plants are saved from lightning, gale and storm,
While heavy structures are thrown out of shape and form.

The fishes through the waters all are bred and fed,
Without support of man through trackless wastes are led;
The birds who dwell around find food and dress in time;
When winter's past, unhurt, they sing a thankful rhyme.

The quadrupeds that travel forest, marsh and plain,
Dwell happy, all which shows their rights from God obtain,
Constructing dens by wondrous skill in way and plan,
Provide for rainy days, as if were teaching man.

But when in prime of life man of these takes possession,
Proclaims 't is all his own, keeps them without transgression,
He calls all useful that is made to help men all;
His language here is well,—how shall this next we call?

He says 't is all for man that earth and sea produce,
Supplying precious treasures more than he can use;
But what regard a soul? he says. When e'er man dies,
There's no God to revive the soul above the skies.

With this expression reason never shall agree.
If man is nothing, Heaven is not for him to be,
And God would be unjust to give eternal glory
To man, if he degrades himself, or tells such story.

An infidel admits all useful that exists
For man's good, but annuls his soul and God resists.
Does such a man deserve to be a king of earth,
Or swell with pride and claim his teachings something worth?

If that man had no soul he would be but a brute.
Why brutes stand under him might cause a new dispute.
If power was not him given, the mule might kick at man,
The horse might bridle him and make two-legged span.

What honor can be due a man with such belief,
If he himself brings down to brutes to find relief?
Can he be called the father of a virtuous child?
It pities him, as being but a monster wild.

To urge a father's blessing who denies his soul,
Can face no reason, nor no household can console.
To call him brute, or to attribute such a fame,
Would curse his soul and our Creator's works misname.

It therefore would be best no brutal names to call,
Though many use such talk, which, too, explains their fall.
'T is pitiable! let's pray for them, O Christian friend,
Their eyes might open ere their lives are at an end!

Experience gives the truths, some are exposed each day!
The consequence is an unhappy death—no pay.
And if we teach that suicide's annihilation,
We but mislead our soul and cause more grief, temptation.

That such a man does not believe in God is plain,
He cannot understand—why then should he explain.
World calls man dunce if foolishly h:s treasures spends,
For then he loses credit, also all his friends.

How pitiable it is to doubt, O neighbors dear,
And not investigate, pass life without just fear!
Since souls are made for Heaven, as God and angels tell,
Lose not the tides of grace your hearts with bliss must swell.

This controversy's painful but with right explained—
Not towards pains compared when 'fore his Judge arraigned.
Since reason tells the truth, time should be well employed
To do what God commands,—without this, all is void.

PART V.

A virtuous man is calm, with love obeys God's laws;
His life devout and humble, Heaven's grace he draws;
To perfect yet himself, keeps clean his soul and heart,
Respects all things the Lord was willing to impart.

But to be wise as God, he knows it cannot be,
For Scripture teaches only God's will to man free;
Though there is meditation for man's life entire,
Like holy fathers found, whose works we must admire.

In Scripture will be seen that God is our Creator,
The Heaven's Power, who sent his Son as meditator;
Who is without begin, and who shall never end;
A gracious Father in whom grace and justice blend.

We see that Adam first was man on earth created,
To lead his soul to God by precepts indicated;
How sin deprived his happiness, lost grace and peace,
For Paradise was locked, all blessings hence to cease.

This sentence, spreading yet above all nations' head,
Is softened through the holy mission Jesus led.
If faith surround our hearts, then Satan is subdued,
His fiery dart repelled and quenched by sacred blood.

It shows the Lord on Adam greatest pity took,
When promising a Saviour (reads the holy book);
How penitence and prayers restored his place on high.
His mind was firm no more to sin—would rather die.

The Patriarchs and Prophets, like the stars so clear,
Enlighten all good-willing men upon this sphere;
To keep the promise up, pronounced by God our Lord,
That man's belief should e'er with will of Heaven accord.

Then Moses, being ruler first by God appointed,
Receiving laws and power, had Aaron priest anointed;
God ordered him to build an Ark or Church, up high,
On elevated mountains pointing clouds and sky.

The Church of God, east, west, grew strong, was beautified,
Where holy things subsisted, laws were specified;
With altar well prepared for daily sacrifice,
The faithful prayers to send, with Heaven to compromise.

Man to obey God offered purest lamb or calf,
His soul to cleanse, restore lost time to his behalf;
And keep our sweet expected Saviour dear in mind,
Who sacrificed Him on the cross to save mankind.

This shows God's Church, laws, ministers all must exist,
To govern just and firm, false prophets to resist;
For foes of man, like thorns and thistles, spoil the fruits,
Destroy the buds and heart, if not dug up by roots.

Be careful, man! descend the ladder from above:
Thou wilt find precious roads which lead to God's rich grove.
Pass by dark age, church persecution, victory,
And meet our Saviour's life, a glorious history.

Christ, Second Person of the Holy Trinity,
His wise instruction, deeds of love, humanity;
He being Father dear of poor and rich, all kind,
Provides the Christians light if they His laws will mind.

His life is filled with meekness, grace and charity,
His voice, sweet, amiable, his tone of dignity;
His acts and precepts are His Father's, God our Lord.
Shall He not by us all be equally adored?

A model Jesus is for all the human race,
And often miracles He does, sends special grace:
With all this, sinners, infidels, go their old way,
Till He, the head of justice, crush their mock display.

All Jesus has condemned is visible to-day;
His prophecies well known show justice in His way.
He said, "The Jews shall be despised to end of times,
And, too, dispersed among the nations in all climes."

This curse by Christ upon their race was last applied,
When through their sinful fathers He was crucified;
This must instruct their offspring, Christ God to declare,
Make them embrace His faith, their losses to repair.

Jerusalem was ruined, the temple was destroyed,
As Jesus said before—His word was never void;
The perpetuity of Church he taught and founded,
Is with the clearest truths and facts to-day surrounded.

If man would meditate on what he sees so bright,
God's mysteries would surely give him all the light;
And lead him straight above, leave world behind and dust.
O soul! what wilt thou say, if through thy fault be lost?

O guilty man, can we then seek the field of Heaven?
If we do not repent we cannot be forgiven!
Though if our soul sincerely to our Maker bend,
It shall gain foot, serve Him, no more His name offend.

An impious writer contradicting works Divine,
To use God's words, he knows it must his works refine;
He speaks of Jesus Christ, and Heaven, all God has blessed,
Convincing there's the truth gives man eternal rest.

Voltaire and Rousseau, being infidels in fact,
Admiring Jesus' virtues, wisdom, word and act,
They said, "If Socrates a wise man died on earth,
Christ's death, then, teaches us, a God is He from birth."

Remember those philosophers who God neglect!
Does reason not persuade men all by short reflect,
All do great blasphemy by fighting Providence,
Well knowing all is given by His omnipotence?

Man, is it not absurd to use thy Saviour's name,
To decorate thy poems or some great works of fame;
Consider Him wise, holy, just, a model life,
And not believe His words and be with Him at strife?

Lo, Jesus Christ proclaimed himself the Son of God,
Arose on earth, to draw men from the slavish road;
He who explained his Father's laws, who dwelt on high,
His miracles confirmed His words—none can deny.

Christ must be as He said, or would be an impostor.
Were he not Son of God, our souls He could not foster;
But Heaven and earth announce His wisdom most Divine.
We never can compare, and should enrich His shrine.

Christ's wisdom far surpasses savants, on this earth;
'T is incontestable was God before his birth.
Shall we deny his Father's word—eternity?
Then lost we are and lost by sins and vanity.

Incorrigible men will lose all Heaven's right.
In former times God's sons withdrew from them in spite;
And Christ himself announced, that trees not bearing fruits,
Shall be cut up and thrown in fire with tops and roots.

God's justice must exist, good works will be rewarded;
He who rebels 'gainst Heaven, sad punishment's accorded.
If man on earth with love obey the Lord's own will,
We see his household bloom, with bliss increasing still.

When many sick were cured, the dead out tombs arose,
Christ clearly spoke the word those wonders to expose;
And yet more signs were asked, but Jesus sees man's thought,
Said, "You shall have no signs but those that Jonas taught."

The prophet Jonas, born and raised in Galilee,
To Ninive was sent to show men's vanity;
Said, "Your sins hurt the Lord and penance must do all,
Or Ninive in forty days in woe will fall."

Lord Jesus, poor on earth, was cursed by men of pride;
His first day being known, He came not to deride;
His holy doctrine clear and pure He well explained;
His virtues won all hearts if not by vice detained.

His counsels sweet consoled men overcome with grief,
His works most laudable gave always great relief ;
His heart inflamed by love intent souls to redeem,—
Shall we not Jesus Christ as model sweet esteem?

Men knew that they were wrong denying clearest light;
Refused submission, sinful rules they tried to hide.
Though all admitted never man that spoke as Christ,
Yet they condemned His works, His counsels, too, despised.

Now eighteen hundred years are passed, yet God shows clear,
Since Adam's fall He offered His Son Jesus dear;
But all should understand His justice must prevail,
To bless the faithful men and punish those who fail.

He that rejects his God rejects all right and truth,
Good teacher he is not—he would mislead the youth;
His aim is to deceive, and lead to great despair,
Oh, what a pity to have children in his care!

The Lord sees deeply into hearts if clear or dim;
He knows his servants well, and those denying Him.
All men who hear the gospel should receive His light;
But when His clemency's abused, day turns to night.

Our Lord his doctrines taught, distinct and openly,
"Those not with Me," He said, "will be opposed to Me;"
Repeating these few words to be well understood,
Because He claimed man's soul—we know it cost His blood.

He called us brothers, sisters, all in His own name,
If we fulfill God's laws by holy acts and fame.
He said, There is no fear for happiness of man:
If he adopt God's will His Heaven he shall obtain.

His child He recommends for infidels to pray,
Because all souls He loving asks with Him to stay.
To-day His flock exists; the Church, He says, is mine,
And disobedient men all walk beyond her line.

The Church of Jesus Christ, the source of bliss for man,
Where through all ages rest God's covenant and plan;
Where words dictated were by Holy Ghost to all,
This is the Church of Rome, we model church must call.

Infallible the Church is, like her head Divine,
And blooming flowers she sends to beautify His shrine;
Hear Jesus' words—"Behold I am with you all days,
E'en to the consummation of the world"—He says.

Where Jesus' Church is built the key of Heaven is there,
The door to open, keep good Christians full in care;
And power is left to burst the fetters of man's sin,
Enjoy communion, and become God's child again.

The doctrine of His Church is as the sun and moon,
Unchanged, and shines in time for faithful late and soon;
It teaches Godly law and rules for souls' salvation.
Alas, who disobey will find poor consolation!

And hence the Lord himself will strengthen humble hearts,
Support his holy Church when built and where it starts;
For 't is the only source whence man can be instructed,
T' obtain that Heaven, whose road before was all obstructed.

There it is well explained man's duty through this law,
What there must be observed, from sins man to withdraw;
That through obedience he enters God's rich home,
But by rebellious acts is plunged in Satan's dome.

We see that God's great word surpasses heavens and earth.
All must obey, because all through His will took birth.
And what enriches earth is gift to man's support—
To-day is he in need the Lord is his resort.

False prophets, heresy, will come, assault God's word,
By shameful doctrines 'gainst the Church of Christ our Lord;
But God's true children watching firm without dismay,
While Heaven protects them all, His Church yet stands to-day.

It cannot be, to bring all Jesus' deeds to light,
For numerous they were as heaven's stars at night;
But all those known are full of love and charity,
Man to procure a glorious eternity.

His model ways must penetrate all upright hearts,
To imitate, since from Him happiness imparts;
Man teaching Jesus' creed, no doubt obtains His grace,
To lead a holy life and Him in Heaven to praise.

Behold, without this grace, death fearful is to men!
An atheist this denies, but we see now and then
Some not depart in peace, but through inhuman act
Destroy themselves or try,—this often is the fact.

The infidels condemn the works of Christian friend,
Whose life is virtuous and fears God to offend,
And recommends each child to serve our Lord above,
His parents weak and old well to support and love.

They yet commit more crime, God's name they scandalize,
Discard His works, which they should note and realize;
And in the least misfortune curse that Holy Name,
Although denying Christ—why then that Name defame?

They plot low stories, God and Scripture to deny;
But say, in Satan's tongue, It is not so—we lie.
The Devil, jealous, knows his God exists, his Lord,
Although he bids his slaves deny Him, mock His word.

Believing not in God, yet dangers make them call;
Then prayers are cast in fear, but not before at all.
We know God's power and justice, shown the world around:
Whole cities are destroyed if not ten just are found.

Here are the truths and facts, protection is in vain;
The buildings strong of iron, stone, shall not remain;
The fire will swing its way in spite of efforts fair,
Destroy what's made by man, for sin can nothing spare.

Yea, many of these facts instruct us night and day;
But we must live for God, to understand His way,
Or what we hear and see 't will serve us to deny.
If our hearts are corrupt, how will we Heaven espy?

Man feels great things unseen descending from on high,
And, being immaterial, shall never die.
The soul is then a spirit given to man in trust,
Which God in Heaven expects—it will not turn to dust.

If God was dwelling here among men on this earth
They might consider Him to be of equal birth;
But man shall not his Maker see 'fore entering Heaven;
His eyes would be too weak—the fact has once been given.

When Jesus was on earth He was true God to all;
His sacrifice was great, though faith of Jews was small;
But when transfigured was on Tabor's holy ground,
No eyes to view his glory strong enough were found.

The projects of an infidel can do no good,
For he opposes Christ, the kernel of man's food.
Although the soul possesses lasting life for man,
It needs Divine precepts full happiness t' obtain.

A nation which rejects the doctrine Jesus taught
Loses God's peace, which through gold cannot be re-bought;
The cities great, where precious gifts were sent within,
Were stripped of happiness when ruled by men of sin.

See Rome, where Peter space obtained Christ's Church to found!
Although a heathen place, conversion spread around;
Then blessings bloomed and scientific arts reflected.
But, once denied, the ruin of Rome is full expected.

Behold, kings, emperors who had attacked that Church
Lost power, were exiled, struggled hard in fiendish clutch.
Some tried returning under her most holy wings;
Could not succeed, belonging to ungodly rings.

When once God's sweetest offerings so bad abused,
The life of man to lowest grade will be reduced;
His poor soul, passing then as through a broken strain,
Is filthy, ever must in Satan's claws remain.

THE END.

www.ingramcontent.com/pod-product-compliance
Lightning Source LLC
Chambersburg PA
CBHW030710110426
42739CB00031B/1635